EASY BAROQU   S
— FOR —
CLASSICAL GUITAR

Compiled and edited by Jerry Willard

A superb collection of delightful music of the Baroque,
arranged in standard notation and tablature.

Amsco Publications
New York/London/Paris/Sydney/Copenhagen/Berlin/Tokyo/Madrid

Cover art: *Mezzetin* by Jean Antoine Watteau, oil on canvas (Getty Images)
Project Editor: David Bradley
Interior design and layout: Len Vogler

Order No. AM 1000494
International Standard Book Number: 978-0-8256-3743-8
HL Item Number: 14037634

Exclusive Distributor for the United States, Canada, Mexico and U.S. possessions:
Hal Leonard Corporation
7777 West Bluemound Road, Milwaukee, WI 53213 USA

Exclusive Distributors for the rest of the World:
Music Sales Limited
14-15 Berners Street, London W1T 3LJ England
Music Sales Pty. Limited
20 Resolution Drive, Caringbah, NSW 2229, Australia

Printed in the United States of America by
Vicks Lithograph and Printing Corporation

Contents

Introduction

The Baroque period of music flourished in Europe from 1600 to 1750, and began with Italian composers such as Claudio Monteverdi (1567–1643), Benedetto Marcello (1686–1739) and Antonio Vivaldi (1678–1741) and culminated with Johann Sebastian Bach (1685–1750) and George Frideric Handel (1685–1759). Baroque music is represented by a singleness of mood and gesture, rhythmic continuity, polyphonic texture, and melodic ornamentation.

Easy Baroque Pieces for Classical Guitar is meant to be an introduction for the beginner and intermediate guitarist to Baroque music. I have tried to select the most beautiful examples of music of the Baroque and, at the same time, tried to use music that is accessible and playable for the advanced beginner and intermediate guitarist.

Ornamentation

One of the most challenging aspects of playing Baroque music is ornamentation. On the guitar, ornaments are done with the left hand using *slurs* (hammer-ons and pull-offs), or with the right hand using cross-string voicings called *campanellas*. Both require a great deal of work and strengthening of hands before they can be properly executed. Therefore, in order to keep this book accessible to the advanced beginner and intermediate guitarist, I have kept ornamentation to a minimum.

There are four main types of ornaments used in this book:

The mordent

 *executed:*  *or:*

The inverted mordent

 *executed:*  *or:*

The trill, starting on the lower note

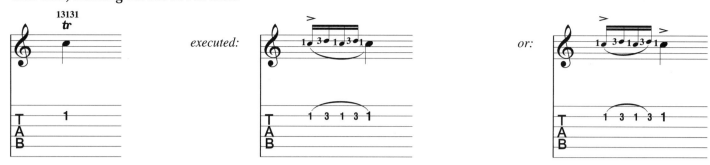

The trill, starting on the upper note

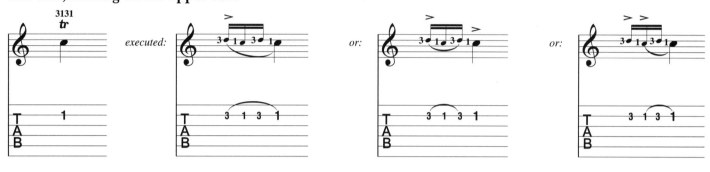

If there is a bass note with the ornament, it will always begin with the first note of the ornament:

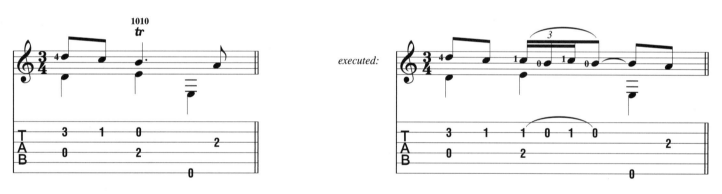

In general, in the Baroque period, all trills, and especially *cadential* trills (occurring at the end of a phrase) begin on the *auxiliary* (or upper) note. The only exception to this is in Spanish Baroque guitar music, represented in this book by Gaspar Sanz (1640–1710) and Santiago de Murcia (1673–1739), where the trill begins on the *fundamental* (lower) note. The Iberian Peninsula was isolated from the rest of Europe, which contributed to the development of a somewhat separate musical language. Also, a great deal of the Spanish Baroque guitar repertoire was based on folk dances and popular songs of the day, and beginning the trill on the lower note is more natural and fitting to this repertoire.

Notes Inégale

In the Baroque period, composers often did not write out the rhythms exactly as they were played. This was true throughout Europe but it was especially ubiquitous in France, where composers and musicians used a style of rhythm called *notes inégale* ("unequal notes"). In the inégale style of playing, the melodic notes were lilted and swung slightly, giving the music a regal feel. The degree of inequality of the rhythms, from heavily dotted to barely noticeable, was usually left to the performer as a matter of taste and expression.

In the Rondeau by Jean-Jospeh Mouret (1682–1738), this is obvious:

Rondeau as written:

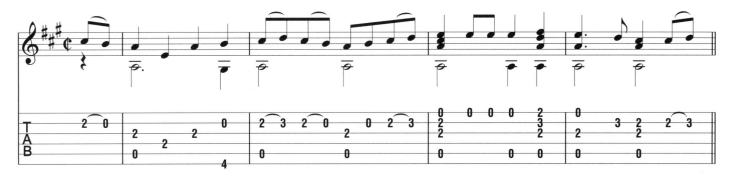

Rondeau as played inégale:

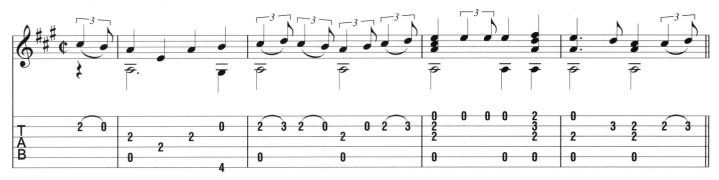

Another example is the Passacaille by Robert de Visée (1650–1725), where I have used inégale only in diatonic or scale-like passages, but not on the intervallic skips, as was the convention:

Passacaille as written:

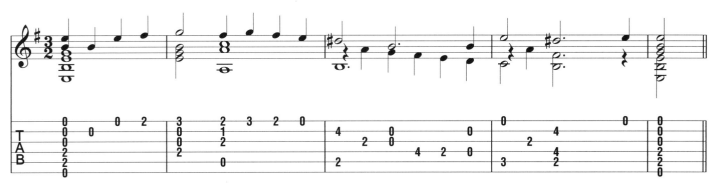

Passacaille as played inégale:

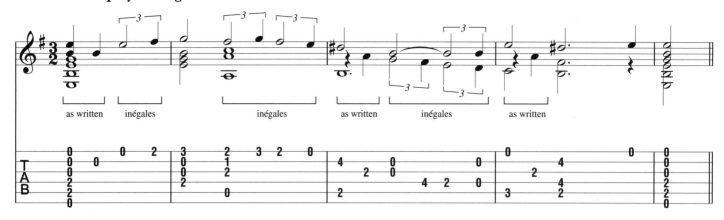

This looks much more complicated than it actually is. Listening to the enclosed CD will help you to acquire the inégale style of playing.

I have recorded inégale on the enclosed CD only where I felt it was absolutely necessary for the proper interpretation of the music that was in obvious French style. In the case of the two Menuets in D Major by Robert de Visée, I recorded the music first in straight rhythm and then inégale on the repeats to show the difference in the two styles.

The guitar lends itself beautifully to the Baroque style of playing. It is no wonder that the guitar has such a rich heritage of Baroque guitar literature from this era. It is my hope that this book will introduce more guitarists to the beauty and intricacies of Baroque music.

Jerry Willard
New York City, April 2010

Easy Baroque Pieces
for
Classical Guitar

Air

Anonymous

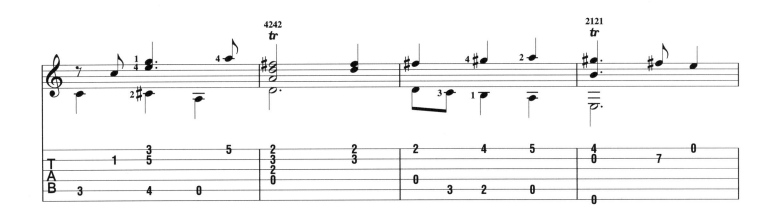

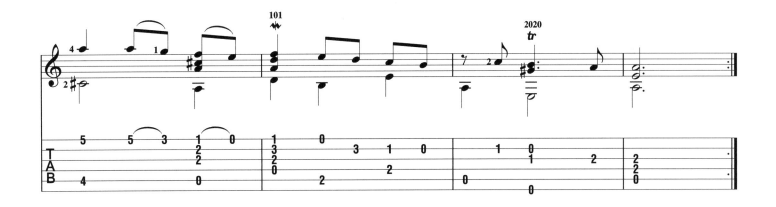

Ciaccona

Anonymous

Bourrée
(from the Fourth Cello Suite)

Johann Sebastian Bach

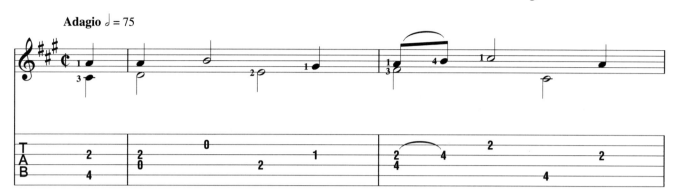

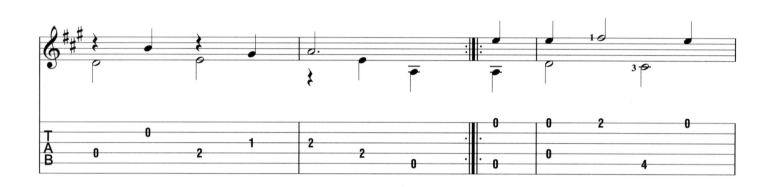

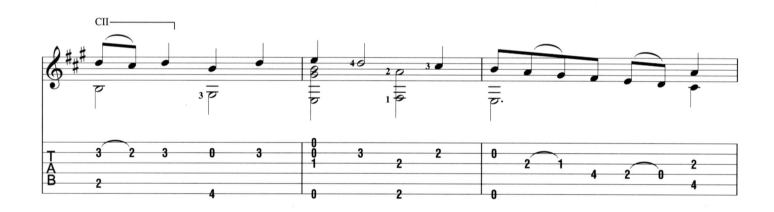

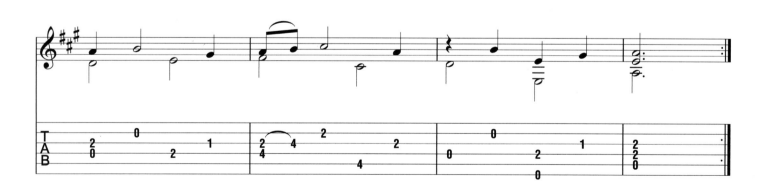

Aria
(from the *Anna Magdelena Notebook*)

Johann Sebastian Bach

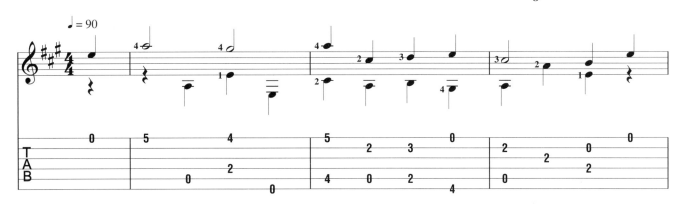

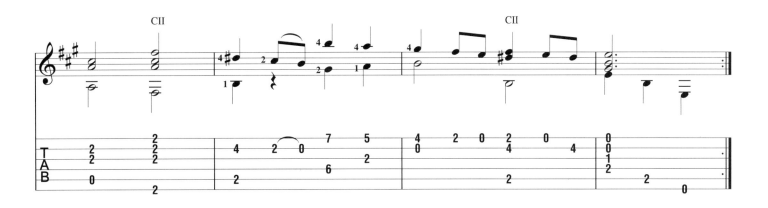

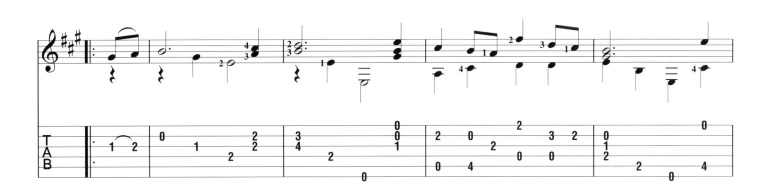

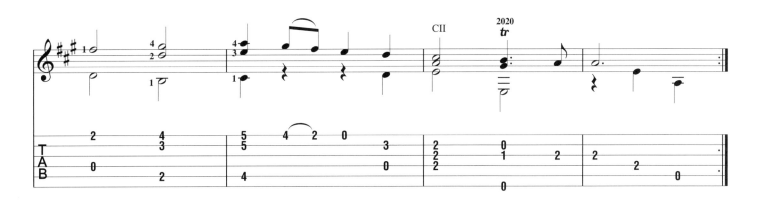

Bist du bei mir

(Be Thou with Me, from the *Anna Magdelena Notebook*)

Johann Sebastian Bach

Menuett in G
(from the *Anna Magdelena Notebook*)

Johann Sebastian Bach

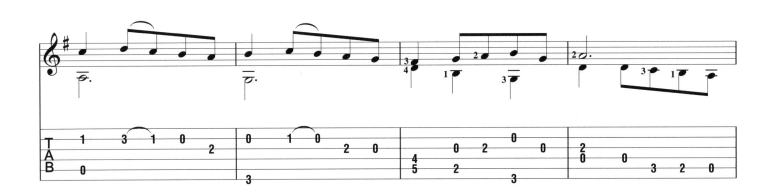

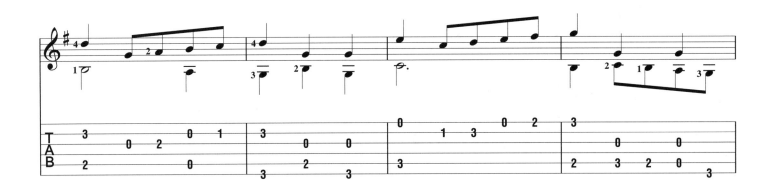

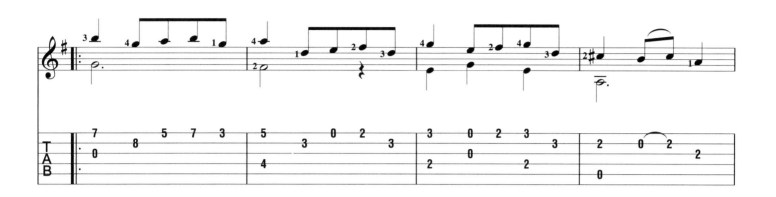

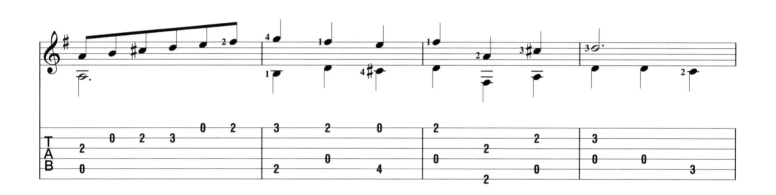

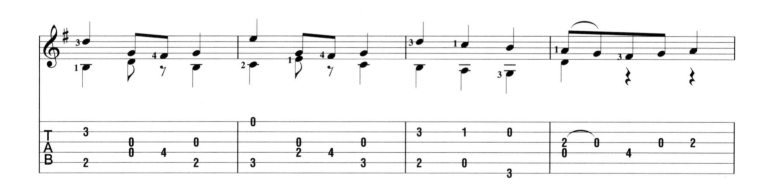

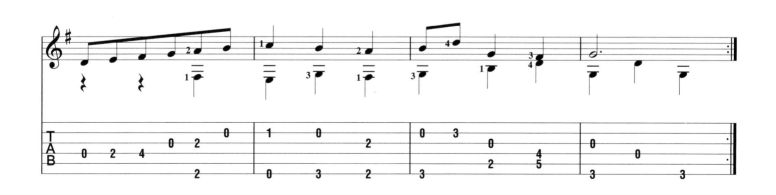

Menuett in A Minor
(from the *Anna Magdelena Notebook*)

Johann Sebastian Bach

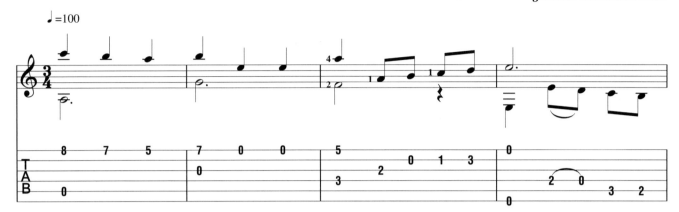

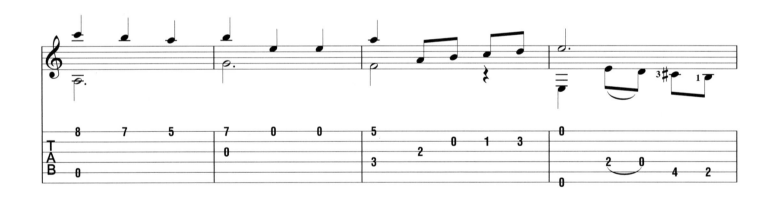

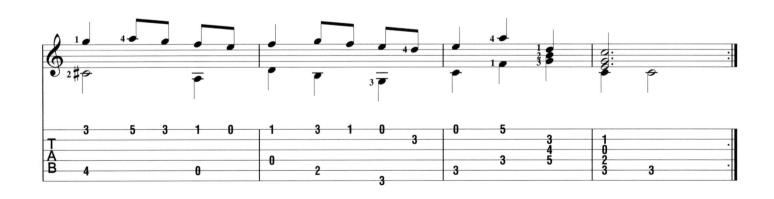

Theme from

Bourrée in A Minor

(from the Second Violin Partita)

Johann Sebastian Bach

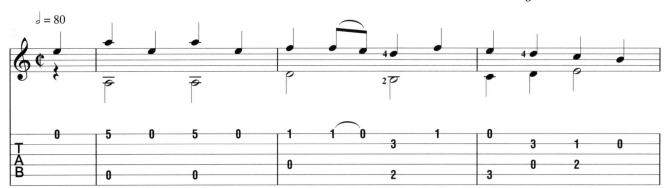

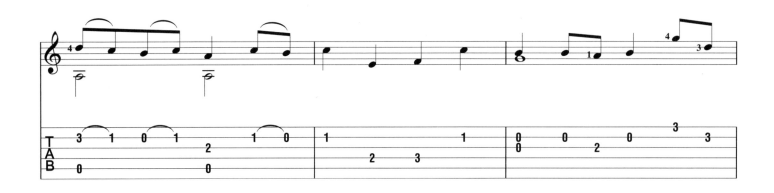

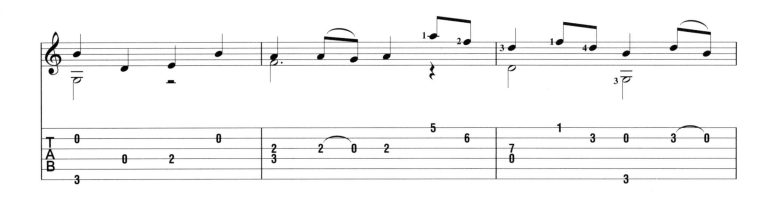

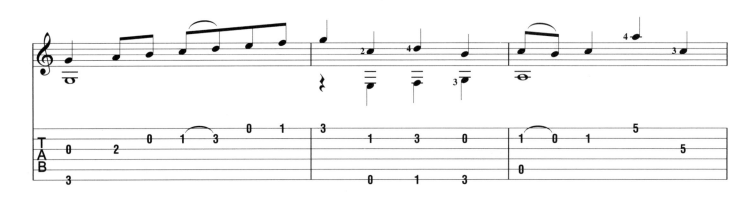

Musette
(from the *Anna Magdelena Notebook*)

Johann Sebastian Bach

Theme from

Gavotte
(from the Third Violin Partita)

Johann Sebastian Bach

Gavottes 1 & 2
(from the Sixth Cello Suite)

Johann Sebastian Bach

Gavotte 1

Gavotte 2

Musette

D.C. Gavotte 1 al Fine

30

O Haupt voll Blut und Wunden

(O Sacred Head, Sore Wounded; from the St. Matthew Passion)

Johann Sebastian Bach

Theme from
Jesu, Joy of Man's Desiring

Johann Sebastian Bach

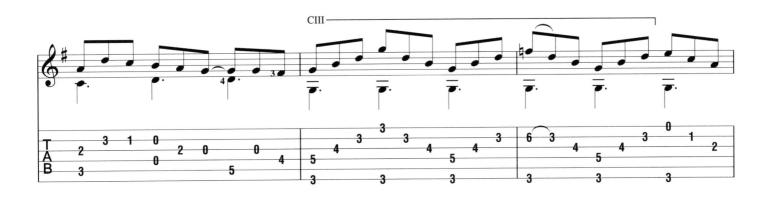

Theme from

Sheep May Safely Graze

(from the Hunting Cantata)

Johann Sebastian Bach

Largo

Arcangelo Corelli

Theme from
Sarabande

George Frideric Handel

Theme from
The Harmonious Blacksmith

George Frideric Handel

Menuett

Johann Krieger

Prelude

Johann Anton Logy

Aria

Sarabande

Johann Anton Logy

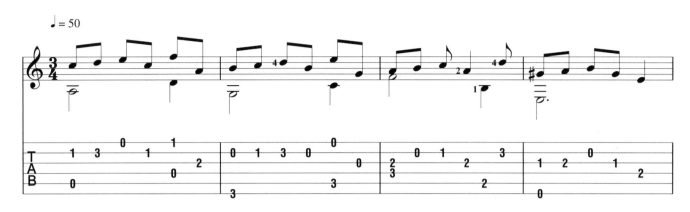

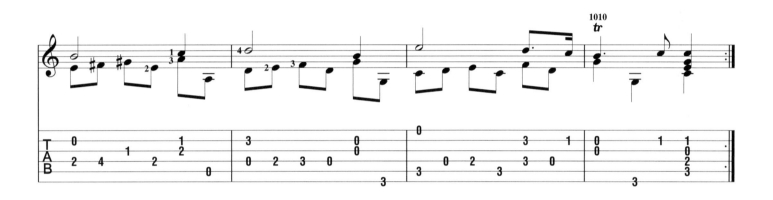

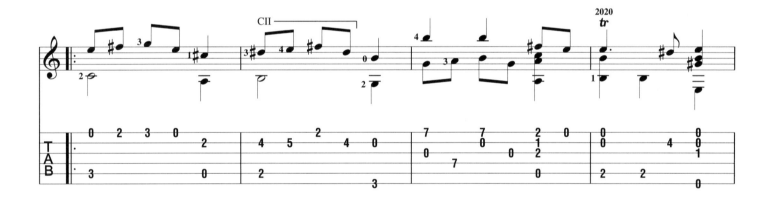

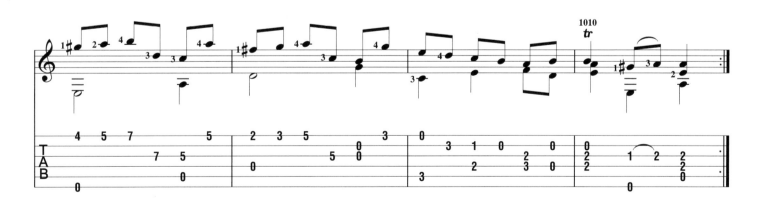

Rondeau

Jean-Joseph Mouret

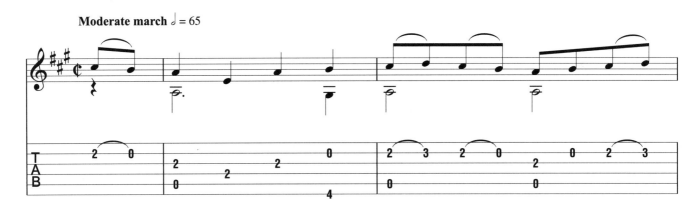

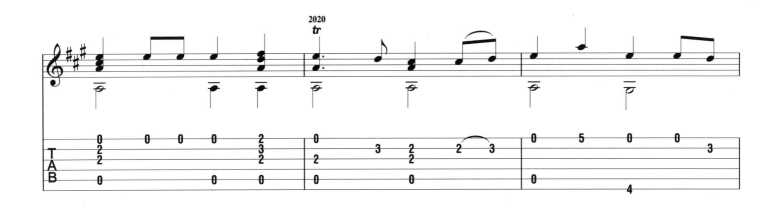

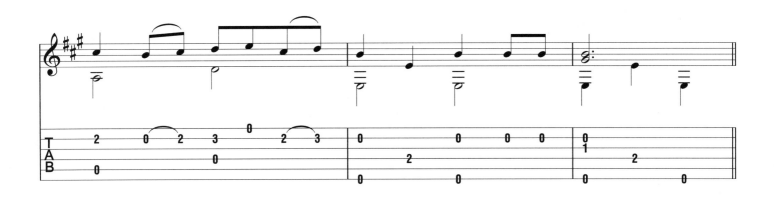

Theme from
Canon

Johann Pachelbel

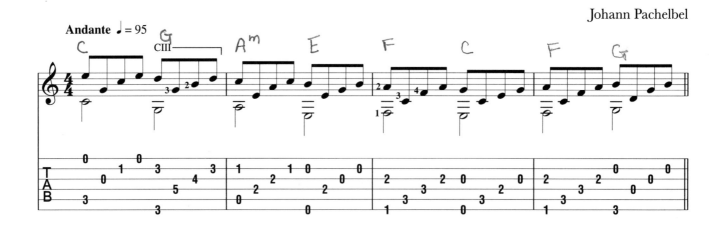

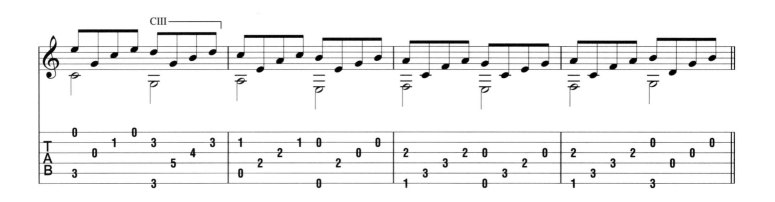

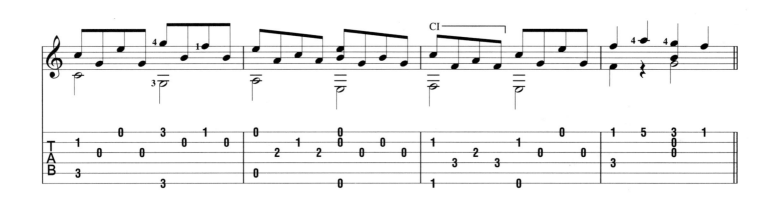

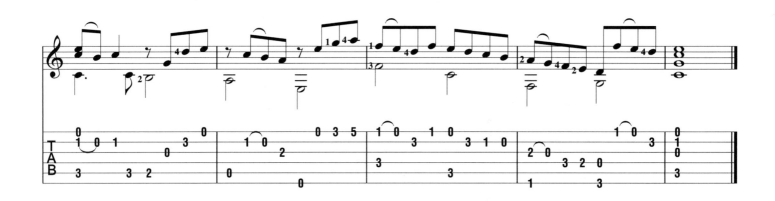

Minuet

Henry Purcell

Minuet

Henry Purcell

La Tia y la Sobrina

Santiago de Murcia

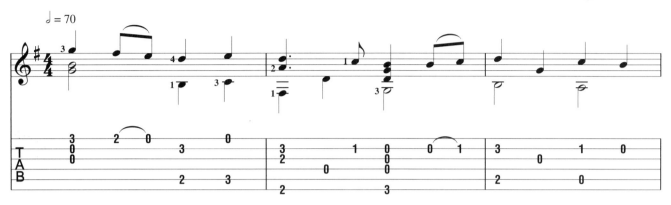

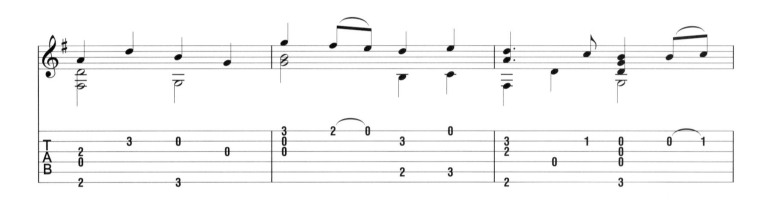

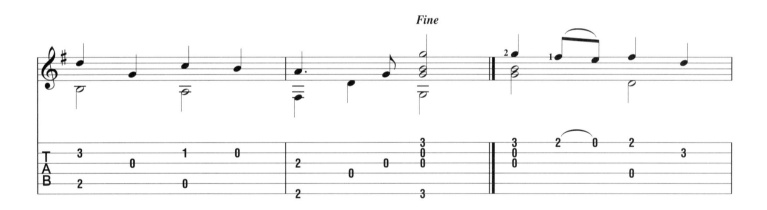

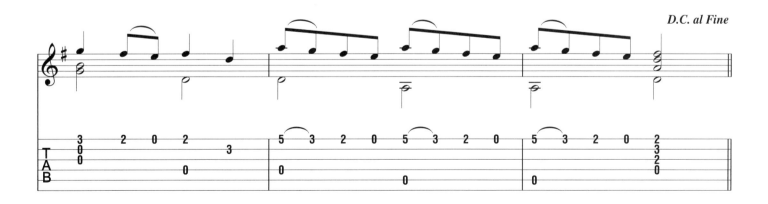

Grave

Santiago de Murcia

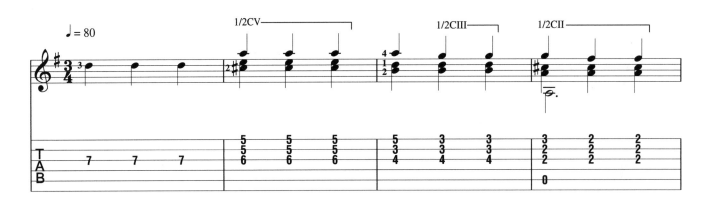

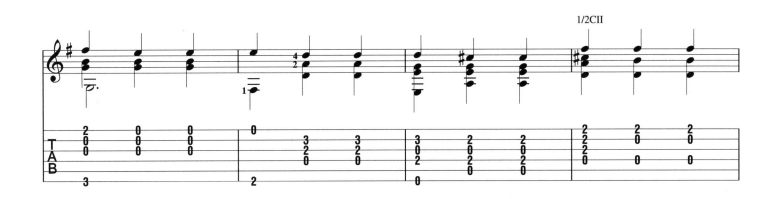

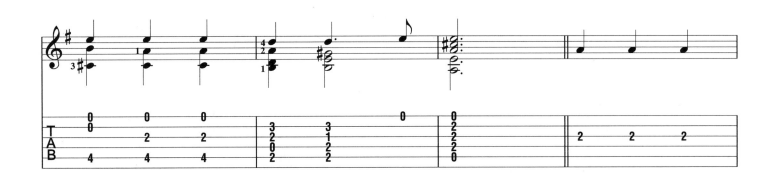

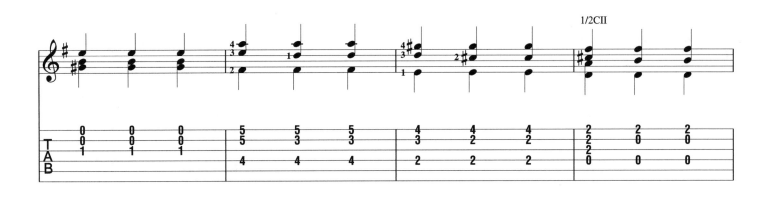

Españoleta

Gaspar Sanz

Lantururú

Gaspar Sanz

Canciones

Gaspar Sanz

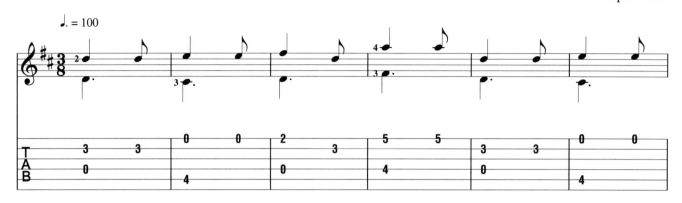

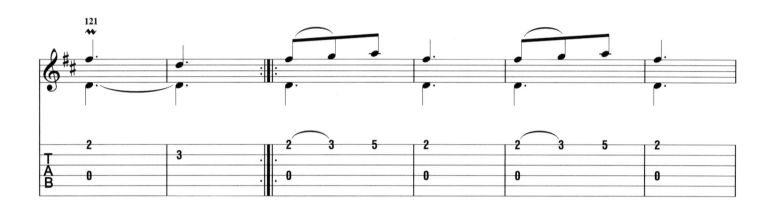

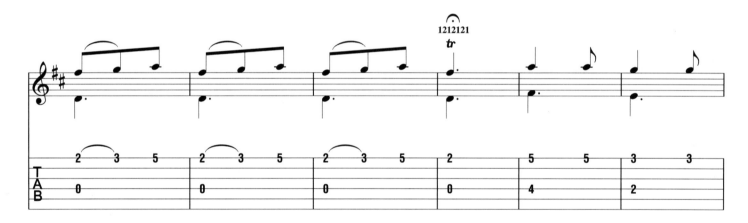

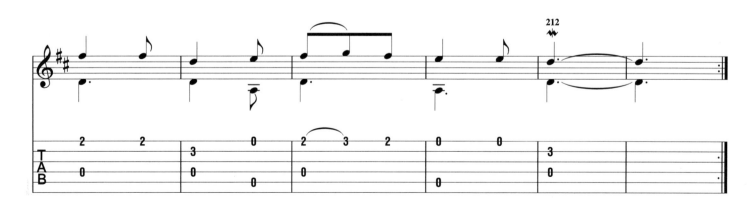

La Miñona de Cataluña

Gaspar Sanz

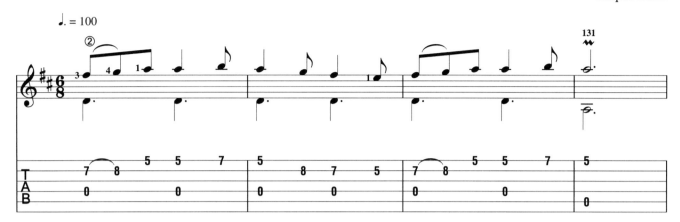

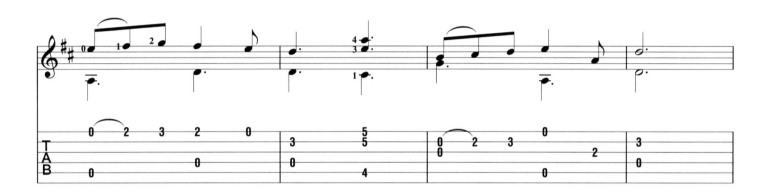

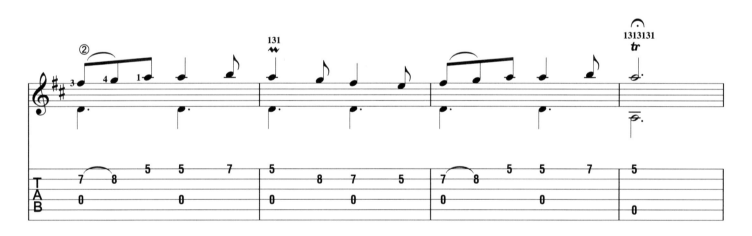

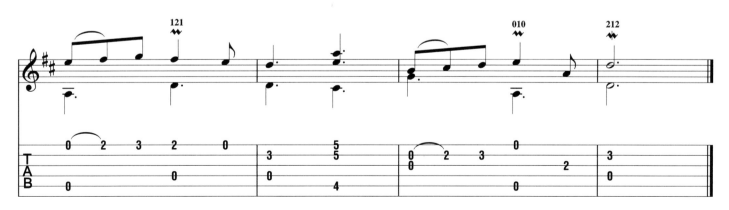

Clarín de los Mosqueteros del Rey de Francia

Gaspar Sanz

La Esfachata de Nápoles

Gaspar Sanz

Rujero

Gaspar Sanz

Paradetes

♩ = 180

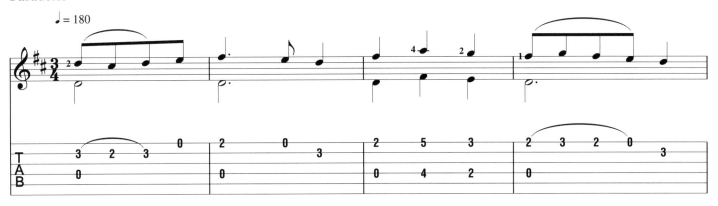

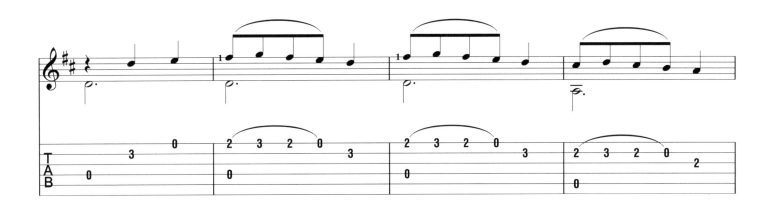

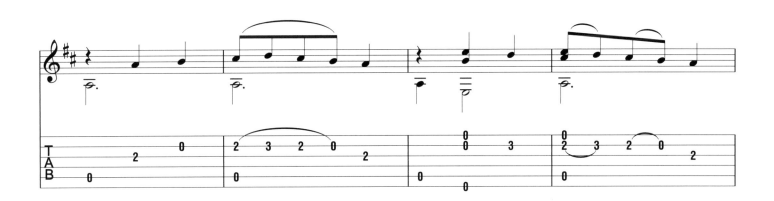

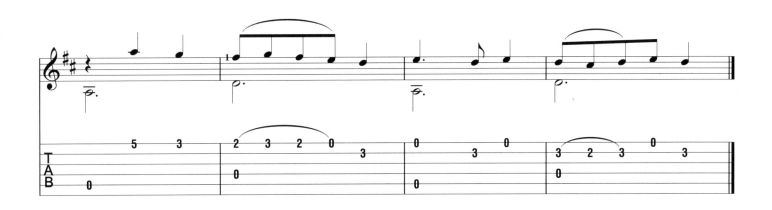

Dance de las Hachas

Gaspar Sanz

Dos Trompetas de la Reina de Suecia

Gaspar Sanz

La Cavallería de Nápoles con dos Clarines

Gaspar Sanz

Theme from
Canarios

Gaspar Sanz

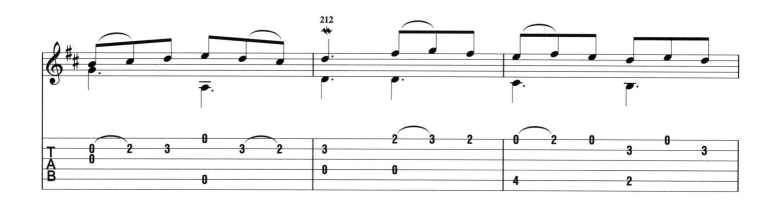

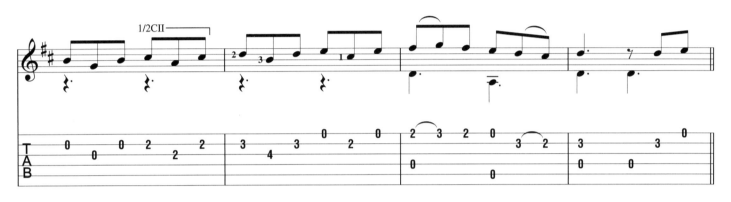
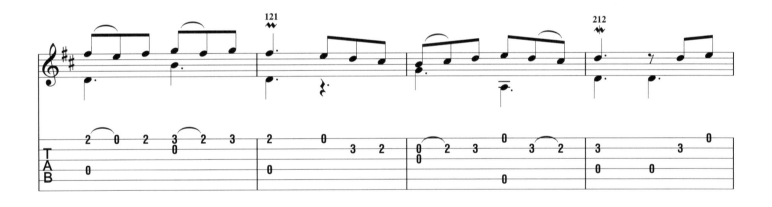
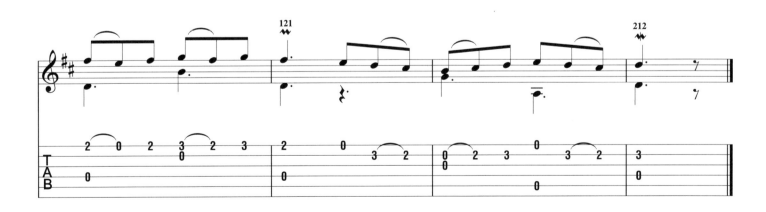

Allemande

Johann Hermann Schein

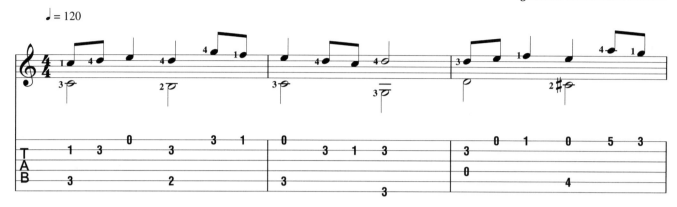

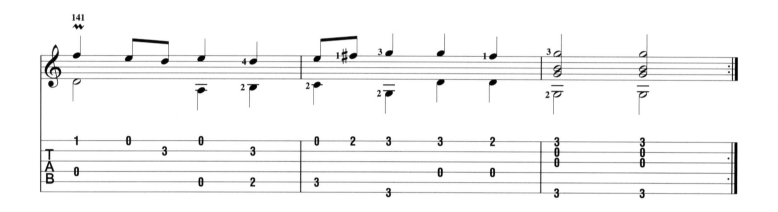

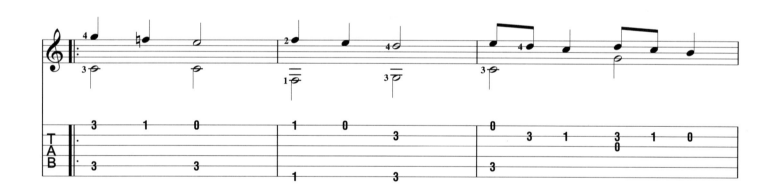

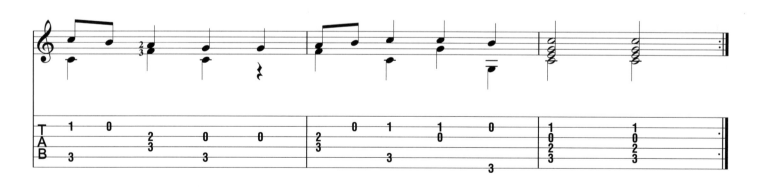

Aria

Daniel Speer

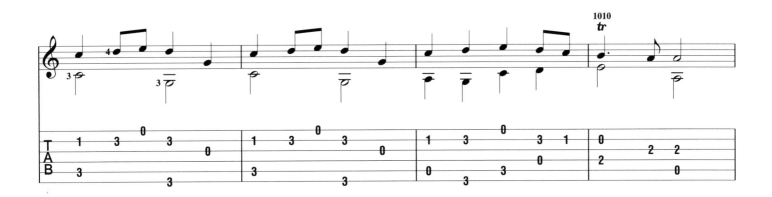

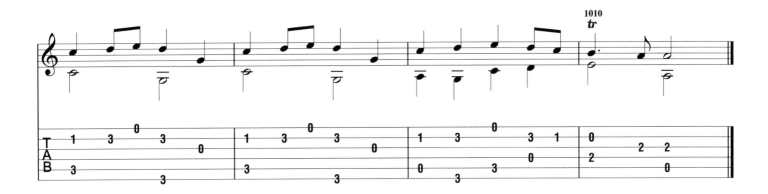

Gavotto

Daniel Speer

Gavotte

Georg Philipp Telemann

Menuet in D Major

Robert de Visée

Prelude in D Minor

Robert de Visée

Menuet in D Major

Robert de Visée

Menuet in E Minor

Robert de Visée

Passacaille

Robert de Visée

Theme from

Largo

(from the Lute Concerto in D Major)

Antonio Vivaldi

Menuett

Silvius Leopold Weiss

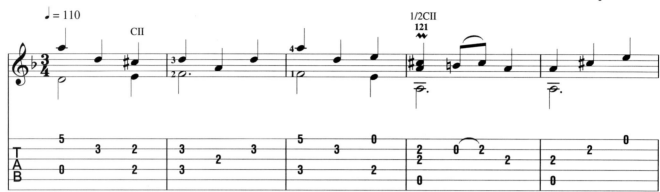

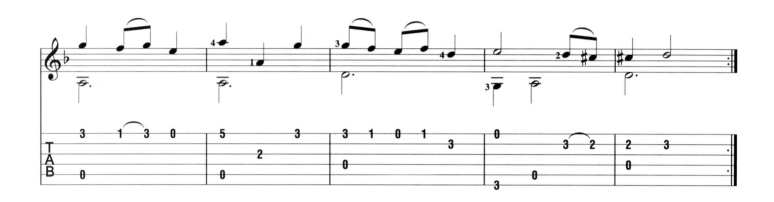

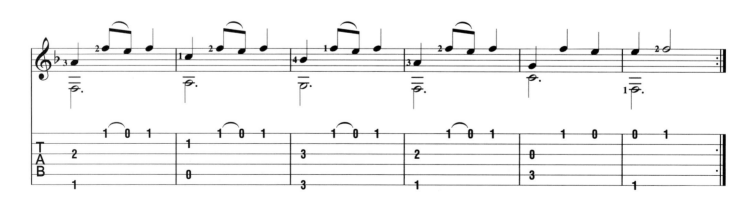

Sarabande

Giovanni Zamboni

Prelude

Giovanni Zamboni

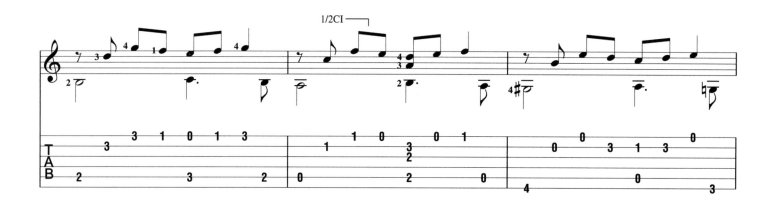

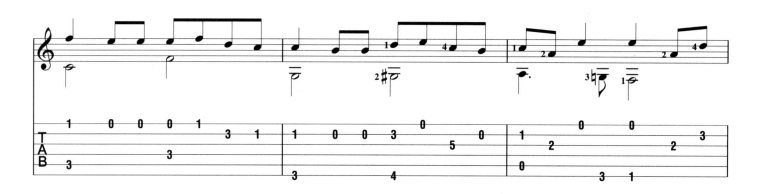

Gavotte

Giovanni Zamboni